CAUSES

CREATIVE ✿ EDUCATION

THE WAR ON TERROR

BY TERESA WIMMER

Published by Creative Education
P.O. Box 227, Mankato, Minnesota 56002
Creative Education is an imprint of The Creative Company
www.thecreativecompany.us

Art direction by Rita Marshall
Design and production by The Design Lab
Printed by Corporate Graphics in the United States of America

Photographs by Alamy (INTERFOTO), AP Images (Sayyid Azim),
Corbis (Bettmann, David Rubinger), DefenseImagery (Staff Sgt.
Michael B. Keller), Getty Images (AFP, Terry Ashe/Time & Life
Pictures, Jaafar Ashtiyeh/AFP, Peter C. Brandt, Martyn Hayhow/
AFP, Mandel Ngan/AFP, Robert Nickelsberg, Richard Nowitz, Office
of the Presidency of the Islamic Republic of Iran, Warrick Page,
Joe Raedle, Stefan Rousseau/Pool, David Silverman, David
Silverman/Newsmakers, Christophe Simon/AFP, StockTrek, Tom
Stoddart), iStockphotos (Andrew Robinson, Oleg Zabielin)

Library of Congress Cataloging-in-Publication Data
Wimmer, Teresa.
Causes / by Teresa Wimmer.
p. cm. — (War on terror)
Includes bibliographical references and index.
Summary: An examination of events that helped create the ongoing
war against Islamic extremists, from early-20th-century Western
imperialism in the Middle East through escalating terrorist attacks.
ISBN 978-1-60818-097-4
1. War on Terrorism, 2001-2009—Juvenile literature. 2. Terrorism—Middle East—Juvenile literature. 3. Islamic fundamentalism—
Juvenile literature. 4. Europe—Relations—Middle East—Juvenile
literature. 5. Middle East—Relations—Europe—Juvenile literature.
6. Imperialism—Juvenile literature. I. Title. II. Series.

HV6431.W5663 2011
909.83'1—dc22   2010033628

CPSIA: 110310 P01387

First Edition
9 8 7 6 5 4 3 2 1

TABLE OF CONTENTS

Many Islamic fundamentalists are willing to blow themselves up in the name of their beliefs, making them unusually dangerous enemies.

I n the late 1980s, a conflict rooted in terrorism began to rear its head on a global scale. This strife pitted Islamic fundamentalists, radical religious **militants** springing primarily from nations in the Middle East, against the countries and culture of the Western world. Spilling across parts of four decades, this conflict—which came to be known from the Western perspective as "The War on Terror"—grew from bombings and guerrilla combat into the first large-scale war of the 21st century, marked by the infamous events of September 11, 2001, and intensive military campaigns in the countries of Afghanistan and Iraq.

Yet the War on Terror did not emerge from nothing—deeply rooted beliefs and actions taken by both Western governments and people of the Middle East and parts of Asia throughout the past century helped fan the flames of conflict. In the early 1900s, the disintegration of a once-great Islamic empire and the rise of Western involvement in Arab countries caused many people in the Middle East to call for change and a return to power centered around the religion of Islam. Most used peaceful means to try to reach their goals, but toward the end of the century, some **extremists** began to resort to violent tactics. These groups inspired many to fight for their cause and many others, especially in the West, to view them as terrorists and murderers.

CHAPTER ONE

FIGHTING WESTERN DOMINATION

At the beginning of the 20th century, maps of the Middle East looked very different than they do today. Much of the area was under the control of the Ottoman Empire, an Islamic empire that had ruled the land for 600 years and was home to some of the world's leading religious scholars, physicians, and scientists. However, by the beginning of the 18th century, the world learned of new advancements in science and the arts primarily from Europeans, who were usually of the Christian faith. At the close of World War I (1914–1918), the Ottoman Empire was dismantled, and the victorious Western allies divided up these largely Arab lands amongst themselves. This was the beginning of a new era of trouble between the Middle East and the West.

When the Western allies carved out countries from the former Ottoman Empire, they did not consider the ethnic differences between peoples of the region, and tribes often found themselves living next to other tribes with whom they did not get along. Many Arab Islamic countries, such as Syria and Lebanon, felt violated by the European powers, who often took possession of an area, used its resources, and promised

PONTUS EUXINUS Hodie MARE NIGRUM.
CARA DENGHIZ Turcis ZORNO MORE Ruffis
CZARNO MORSE Polonis MAURO THALASSA Græcis
DAS SCHWARTZE MEER.

MARE MEDITERRANEUM

MARE LYBICUM

MARE ASIATICUM

MARE CASPIUM Sive HYRCANUM

MARE ARABICUM

MAGNI
TURCARUM DOMINATORIS
IMPERIUM
per

Although still powerful, the Ottoman Empire began to weaken in the 1700s, a time that historians have called its "stagnation" period.

democracy to the people of that country but failed to deliver. The result of this division of lands, according to American historian David Fromkin, was the creation of a "group of neighboring countries that have not become nations even today."

Islam plays a central role in all aspects of the daily lives of Muslims, and many Muslims were fearful that their religion would come to an end as Western influence grew. In response, groups such as the Muslim Brotherhood, created by an Egyptian schoolteacher named Hassan al-Banna in the 1920s, sprang up to call for a return to Islam's purist roots. From the viewpoint of such fundamentalist groups, the reason that the Ottoman Empire had fallen was that its leaders had moved away from the traditional teachings of Islam and toward **secular** ways. Such Islamic groups—which, in the beginning, advocated using nonviolent means to bring about changes in Islamic governments they saw as corrupt—drew more and more followers throughout the first half of the 20th century.

Hassan al-Banna

Muslims in Palestine burn a Danish flag in 2005 in protest of the *Jyllands-Posten* cartoons depicting the prophet Muhammad.

CONTROVERSIAL CARTOONS

For most Muslims, Islam defines much of their being and is not to be taken lightly. In 2005, the Danish newspaper *Jyllands-Posten* printed 12 cartoons of the prophet Muhammad. A majority of Muslims believe that Muhammad must never be depicted, and the cartoons caused outrage across the Islamic world, spurring rioting in the Middle East and Africa that left embassies and churches burned and more than 100 people dead. Among Europe's growing Muslim population, the incident highlighted the sensitive issue of the importance of balancing free expression with respect for religion.

However, the creation of Israel led some Islamic fundamentalists to believe that violence was necessary to drive Western nations out of Arab lands and restore Islamic power and pride. In 1948, the United Nations (UN) split the Arab land of Palestine and made Israel, which was meant to be, for Jews, a return to their historical homeland. Palestinians protested the loss of their land, and many Muslims were irate at the thought of Israeli Jews, and the Western powers that supported them, in cities such as Jerusalem, which was a holy site for Muslims. To later terrorists, such as al Qaeda leaders Osama bin Laden and Ayman al-Zawahiri, this act violated the rights of the ummah, or worldwide community of Muslims, to control its own destiny and confirmed the West's intent to divide the Muslim world into small, weak states that might be easily controlled.

The formation of Israel led to a long-lasting Arab-Israeli conflict, with Palestine and its Muslim supporters on one side and Israel and its Western (especially British and American) allies on the other. Radicals viewed any Islamic government that cooperated or made peace with Israel as corrupt, and they vowed to wage violent **jihad** to remove such

Jersusalem is a city holy to many; a Russian Orthodox church (foreground) sits near the famed Islamic shrine the Dome of the Rock (background).

ARABS VERSUS ISRAELIS

Since 1948, when the nation of Israel was created, the Arab-Israeli conflict has been at the heart of much of the violence in the Middle East. However, the conflict has had brief periods of peace. The Camp David Accords, signed in 1978 by Egyptian president Anwar al-Sadat and Israeli prime minister Menachem Begin, marked the first time an Arab nation made peace with Israel. The truce, however, provoked outrage among other Arab Muslims and led to Egypt's expulsion from the Arab League in 1979.

Oil has factored prominently into many Middle Eastern conflicts; this photo shows Kuwaiti oil wells burning at the end of the Persian Gulf War.

OIL DEPENDENCE

Many economists have urged the United States to lessen its dependence on foreign oil, including that from the Middle East. In 1970, the U.S. imported 24 percent of its oil; in 2008, it imported nearly 70 percent. America, which makes up less than 5 percent of the world's population, uses 25 percent of its oil. Because of this, recent presidents have placed greater importance on finding alternate sources of energy, such as wind, solar power, and electricity. In 2008, presidential candidate Barack Obama set a goal of zero oil imports from the Middle East by 2018.

governments from power. In 1981, Egyptian president Anwar al-Sadat was assassinated by al-Zawahiri and other Egyptian jihadists for signing a peace agreement with Israeli prime minister Menachem Begin. This act "transformed [al-Zawahiri]," American counterterrorism expert Bruce Riedel stated, "from an agitator and critic of the Egyptian government to a spokesman for revolutionary violence, even if it meant ... murder."

A decade later, new conflict arose. In August 1990, Iraq, under president Saddam Hussein, invaded neighboring Kuwait, aiming to seize its land and oil resources. Other border countries, such as Saudi Arabia, feared Iraqi forces would invade them as well. The Saudi government chose to accept an offer from the U.S. to station American troops in Saudi lands for protection, declining an offer from bin Laden (himself a Saudi) to assist the Saudi government with money and fighters. In response, bin Laden labeled the Saudi government a traitor for allowing **infidels** from the U.S. into the holy Muslim cities of Mecca and Medina, which lie in Saudi Arabia.

In 1991, when Hussein's forces were defeated by a U.S.-led **coalition** in the Persian Gulf War, Hussein was ordered to disarm and allow UN weapons inspectors into Iraq to prove his cooperation. Hussein, however, did not comply. In response, the **UN Security Council** strengthened sanctions, or penalties, on Iraq, which restricted trade and transportation and made it difficult for Iraqi citizens to have access to adequate food, education, and medical care. This angered many Muslims, who criticized the U.S. and allies such as Great Britain for causing much suffering among innocent Iraqi people, especially the country's **Kurdish** population, which was particularly oppressed by Hussein's government.

In the 1990s, al Qaeda and other terrorist groups also accused the West of trying to build up Israel's fighting capabilities. With U.S. support, Israel became one of the preeminent **nuclear** powers in the Middle East, giving it military superiority over the Arab region, despite the West's stated desire to restrict the spread of nuclear weapons. Jihadists began to single out the U.S. as the primary force opposing Islam and Muslims. For al Qaeda, which had emerged in the late 1980s as one of the most prominent jihadist groups, the only way to accomplish its goals—driving the U.S. and other Western nations out of Muslim lands, eliminating Israel, and uniting the ummah under a restored Islamic **caliphate**—was to deploy violence against the West. It soon decided to strike the U.S. at home.

Israel built up a formidable air force by purchasing many fighter jets—such as this F-16, bought in 1980—from the U.S.

KURDISH GENOCIDE

On March 16, 1988, Iraqi military forces, under the direction of Saddam Hussein, used poisonous gas and other chemical weapons against the people of Kurdistan, a region that falls partly in Iraq. Saddam had accused Kurdish militias of cooperating with Iran during the Iran-Iraq War of 1980–1988. The **genocide** killed more than 5,000 civilians and injured another 11,000, becoming one of the largest chemical weapons attacks against a civilian population in history. In November 2006, the Iraqi Interim Government found Hussein guilty of crimes against humanity. He was executed in December 2006.

CHAPTER TWO

THE RISE OF TERROR

Throughout the first half of the 1900s, the U.S. and the West had a largely cooperative relationship with some prominent national governments in the Middle East. That began to change, however, once Israel became a state and jihadist movements gained steam throughout the 1960s and '70s. Western nations were not at first concerned about the growth of radical Islam. However, the Iranian Revolution and the Iran hostage crisis changed that.

In February 1979, revolutionaries took control of Iran's government and forced Mohammad Reza Shah Pahlavi—the unpopular, U.S.-backed Iranian king—into exile in favor of Ruhollah Khomeini, a fundamentalist Islamic **cleric** who promised a return to Islamic rule in Iran. That November, after the U.S. had allowed Pahlavi to seek medical treatment in America, a group of militant Islamic students protested by seizing the U.S. embassy in the city of Tehran and holding 66 American workers hostage, demanding that Pahlavi return to Iran to face punishment for his authoritarian rule. The hostage crisis ended peacefully after 444 days and Pahlavi's death. However, the creation of the Islamic Republic of Iran showed the West that a fundamentalist Islamic government could succeed in modern times, and that it was not above condoning terrorist acts.

THE REFORMER

In the late 1940s, the king of Iran, Mohammad Reza Shah Pahlavi, began keeping oil profits for himself rather than using them to provide public services. In response, reformer Mohammad Mosaddeq led a movement to oust Pahlavi and turn Iran's oil industry over to the national government. After Mosaddeq became prime minister in 1951, U.S. officials overthrew him and restored Pahlavi—who was friendly to America—to power. Mosaddeq was arrested, tried, and convicted of treason by Pahlavi's government. For many people in the Middle East, Mosaddeq came to represent Islam's stand against the West.

Mohammad Reza Shah Pahlavi

BLACK SEPTEMBER

Violence between Palestinians and Israelis began years before Israel was created in 1948 and escalated throughout the 1970s. On September 5, 1972, during the Summer Olympics, eight Palestinian terrorists stormed the living quarters of the Israeli Olympic team in Munich, Germany. The terrorists were from the group Black September, which was believed to be a branch of the Palestine Liberation Organization (PLO)—a group originally dedicated to reclaiming Palestinian land from Israel. When the crisis was over, 11 Israelis were dead, along with 5 terrorists and a German policeman.

The widow of a slain Israeli Olympian views the room in which Black September terrorists began the infamous 1972 Munich massacre.

Iran was only one nation involved in the growing threat of terrorism against the West. In 1983, Hezbollah, a militant group formed to oppose Israel, drove a bomb-filled truck into U.S. Marine barracks in Beirut, Lebanon, killing 241 troops. According to **intelligence** gathered by the U.S., Hezbollah received weapons and financial and political aid from Iran and Syria, two countries that America had previously suspected of harboring terrorists. In December 1988, Libyan terrorists used a planted bomb to blow up Pan American Flight 103, bound from London to New York, over Lockerbie, Scotland, killing all 259 people on board the plane.

Still, up until the 1990s, Islamic terrorism had not struck the U.S. mainland. That changed with the first attack on New York City's World Trade Center. On February 26, 1993, a huge car bomb went off in a parking garage beneath the "Twin Towers," killing 6 people and wounding more than 1,000. U.S. government agencies acted swiftly and apprehended a group of Islamic extremists led by Kuwaiti Ramzi Yousef. The six individuals responsible were tried, convicted, and sentenced in a measure of justice that gave American citizens faith in

U.S. intelligence agencies and their ability to deal with terrorists. However, the attack also represented a frightening expansion of global Islamic terrorism. Yousef later said that the group had hoped to kill about 250,000 people with the attack.

The U.S. did not know at the time that Yousef and his uncle, Khalid Sheikh Mohammed, had ties to al Qaeda. Intelligence officials thought of al Qaeda's leader, Osama bin Laden, as mainly a financier of extremist organizations and not as the brains and inspiration behind this growing trend in terrorism. But the U.S. and the rest of the world soon became aware of bin Laden's powers and hatred of America. On February 23, 1998, bin Laden issued a public **fatwa** in which he and al-Zawahiri proclaimed war on the U.S.

It was "the duty of every Muslim in all countries," bin Laden said, "to kill the Americans and their allies—civilian and military" and to drive the U.S. from the Persian Gulf region.

On the morning of August 7, 1998, al Qaeda orchestrated its first simultaneous attacks on U.S. targets when bomb-laden trucks drove into U.S. embassies at Nairobi, Kenya, and Dar es Salaam, Tanzania. The attacks killed 223 people and injured nearly 5,000 more. Because August is typically a vacation month for American embassy workers, only 12 of those killed were Americans; most of the slain were Africans, some of whom were Muslims. This signal that al Qaeda was prepared to sacrifice Muslims if it meant also harming Americans struck new fear into people worldwide.

Kenyans look at the half-destroyed U.S. embassy in Nairobi after terrorists struck with an explosives-filled truck in a 1998 suicide attack.

CHRISTMAS DAY BOMBING

On December 25, 2009, Nigerian engineering student Umar Farouk Abdulmutallab brought explosives, hidden in his underwear, onto Northwest Airlines Flight 253, which was bound from Amsterdam, Netherlands, to Detroit, Michigan. After passengers saw smoke coming from Abdulmutallab's seat, authorities arrested him in Detroit. Abdulmutallab later admitted to training at an al Qaeda terrorism camp. Although the bomb failed to detonate and the flight concluded safely, U.S. counterterrorism officials were criticized for not having intercepted the terrorist plot.

In response to the American embassy attacks, U.S. president Bill Clinton ordered air strikes against targets in Afghanistan, where bin Laden was believed to be staying, but the terrorist leader escaped before the assault happened. Clinton prepared Americans for the battle against terrorism when he said, in an August 1998 speech, "We will not yield to this threat. We will meet it no matter how long it may take. This will be a long, ongoing struggle between freedom and fanaticism, between the rule of law and terrorism."

Bin Laden and other al Qaeda leaders had found a safe haven in Afghanistan under the protection of the Taliban, an extremist **Sunni** Muslim political organization that had controlled Afghanistan's government since 1996. Many times Clinton sent **diplomats** to talk with such Taliban leaders as Mohammed Omar and demand that they hand over bin Laden. The Taliban repeatedly claimed it did not know bin Laden's location. Similar attempts at negotiation between the U.S. and the president of Pakistan, General Pervez Musharraf, also

U.S. president Bill Clinton

The 1998 air strikes in Afghanistan, called Operation Infinite Reach, represented America's first significant attack against al Qaeda.

ended in failure. Musharraf, who valued the Taliban's support in helping maintain control of his own presidency, refused to provide the U.S. with any information on al Qaeda or the Taliban.

By 2001, it was clear that the Western allies were opposed by a global network of terrorism, one consisting of many different cells, or groups. The U.S. government also realized that diplomacy and attempts to reason with the terrorists would not work. To counter individuals who were stateless and willing to give up their lives as martyrs in the name of Islam and to kill as many Westerners as possible, U.S. intelligence agencies could only hope to sniff out terror plots before they happened. One ambitious plot from the mind of Khalid Sheikh Mohammed, however, went undetected.

On September 11, 2001, a group of 19 al Qaeda terrorists hijacked 4 planes in the U.S. bound from the East Coast to destinations on the West Coast. Two of the planes were deliberately flown into the Twin Towers of the World Trade Center, one struck the **Pentagon** in Washington, D.C., and one crash-landed in a Pennsylvania field after passengers fought back against the hijackers. The attacks collapsed the World Trade Center and killed nearly 3,000 people, becoming the worst assault ever on U.S. soil. In response, the U.S. prepared to unleash the full might of its military. The War on Terror had truly begun.

A fireball erupts from the south tower of the World Trade Center as it is struck by United Airlines Flight 175 on September 11, 2001.

FORT HOOD MASSACRE

The "9/11" attacks prompted U.S. officials to closely monitor links between Americans and Middle Eastern terrorists. In November 2009, Major Nidal Malik Hasan, a U.S. military psychiatrist, opened fire at the Fort Hood army base in Texas, killing 13 people and wounding 42. Afterward, military officials revealed that they had intercepted communications in 2008 between Hasan and Anwar al-Awlaki, a former cleric and spiritual adviser to two of the 9/11 hijackers. Fort Hood witnesses reported having heard Hasan shout "Allahu Akbar" (Arabic for "God is great") during the 2009 massacre.

CHAPTER THREE

TAKING IT TO THE WEST

With the 9/11 attacks on America, al Qaeda achieved its goal of bringing terrorism to the U.S. mainland. The terrorist group hoped the attacks would have a secondary effect, too—that the mass casualties would provoke the U.S. to retaliate by invading Muslim lands. Jihadists could then rally support to oppose the invaders and inflict defeat on the U.S. and its allies, forcing the West out of the Islamic world. Pro-Western Muslim leaders could then be replaced, and Israel, left isolated, could be demolished.

Such were the hopes of leaders such as bin Laden and al-Zawahiri. However, instead of a sweeping, ill-prepared invasion of the Middle East, U.S. president George W. Bush launched a more focused response in the form of Operation Enduring Freedom in Afghanistan in October 2001. The U.S. and such allies as Britain and Australia attacked the Taliban, contributing air power and strategic aid to the Northern Alliance—a multi-ethnic collection of Afghan militias who opposed the Taliban. Within weeks, the Taliban was defeated on the battlefield and removed from power in Afghanistan. Al Qaeda leaders proved more elusive, hiding out in complex cave systems within the country's vast mountains.

The coalition got a boost in the fall of 2001 when General Musharraf turned on

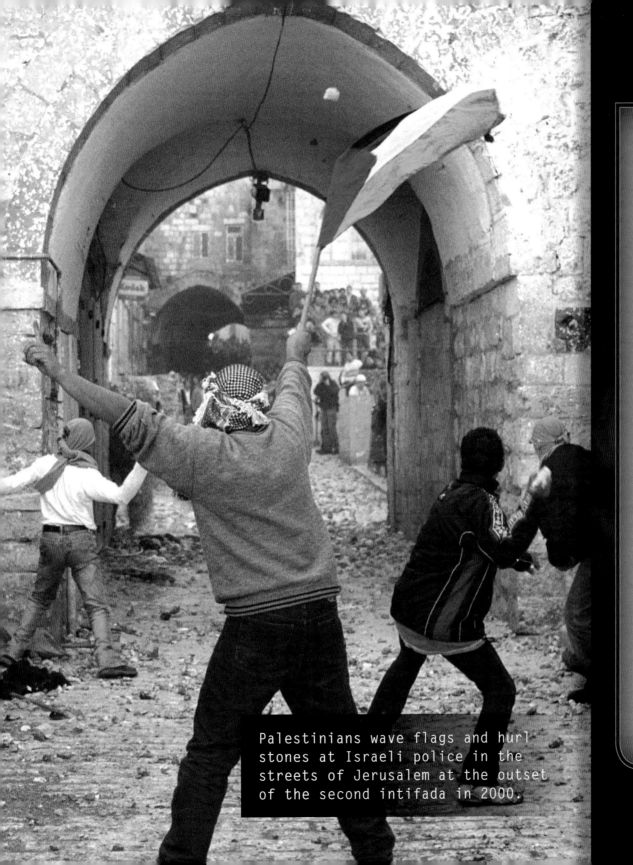

Palestinians wave flags and hurl stones at Israeli police in the streets of Jerusalem at the outset of the second intifada in 2000.

SECOND INTIFADA

In September 2000, Israeli prime minister Ariel Sharon visited a temple in Jerusalem, which is a holy site for both Palestinian Arabs and Israeli Jews. In protest, a group of 1,500 Palestinians shouted insults and threw stones at Israeli troops. Soon, an all-out war (called "intifada" by Palestinians) erupted. Intifada—Arabic for "an uprising"—is an ongoing struggle between Palestinians and Israelis for control of disputed land. The first intifada (1987–1993) and second intifada (2000–2005) resulted in the deaths of more than 7,500 Palestinians and 1,100 Israelis.

his former allies and began cooperating with the coalition. By December 2001, up to 600 al Qaeda members had been captured and more than 200 killed, and many of the remaining Taliban and al Qaeda leaders were isolated along the border between Pakistan and Afghanistan. For al Qaeda, defeat seemed imminent.

However, al Qaeda and the Taliban then caught two breaks. On December 13, 2001, five terrorists from groups associated with bin Laden attacked India's government building in New Delhi. India blamed Pakistan—its neighbor and number-one enemy—for harboring these terrorists and mobilized troops along its border with Pakistan, prompting Musharraf to move his troops from the Afghanistan to the Indian border. Then, in March 2002, the

U.S. began to prepare for a potential attack on Iraq, pulling key intelligence and military forces out of Afghanistan. These diversions of resources would allow al Qaeda to escape and the Taliban to regroup.

Like the U.S., al Qaeda began to turn its attention to Iraq. By the summer of 2002, there was speculation that the U.S.—worried that Iraq might sell **weapons of mass destruction (WMD)** to terrorists—would invade Iraq, and al Qaeda decided to take advantage of this new development. On February 11, 2003, bin Laden sent a letter to the Iraqi people, broadcast on Al-Jazeera (the most prominent independent media network in the Middle East), warning them that the U.S. and its allies were planning to attack Iraq and promoting his West-versus-Islam

Pakistani president Pervez Musharraf

KASHMIR CONFLICT

Much of the conflict today between India and Pakistan revolves around Kashmir, a fertile region located to the north of both countries. When Pakistan was created in 1947 from India, Kashmir had the option of joining either India or Pakistan; Kashmir's leader chose India. However, because the majority of people in Kashmir and Pakistan are Muslim, and most Indian people are not, Pakistan argued that Kashmir should become part of its country. Since 1947, many clashes have taken place between the two nations' militaries.

NEW BELIEFS

In mid-2003, Osama bin Laden directed almost daily car bombings inside Saudi Arabia, a country he saw as corrupt for cooperating with the U.S. However, the attacks failed to disrupt the Saudi government. Instead, the Saudi Ministry of Interior set up a rehabilitation program in 2004 for captured terrorists, in which Saudi clerics attempted to persuade detainees to discontinue their support for al Qaeda. The program was a success. Of the 3,000 prisoners handled between 2004 and 2008, some 1,400 abandoned their jihadist beliefs, and, after being released, fewer than 40 were known to have returned to al Qaeda.

U.S. Marines pulled down a 39-foot-tall (12 m) statue of Saddam Hussein when coalition troops reached the heart of Baghdad in April 2003.

message. Thousands of Arabic volunteer fighters went to Iraq in the next few weeks to begin making preparations to resist the U.S.-led invasion and to work with Abu Musab al-Zarqawi, a longtime associate of bin Laden who would become the leader of al Qaeda in Iraq. Al-Zarqawi—knowing that Iraq's military would not be able to stop the stronger Western forces—prepared for the day *after* Saddam Hussein's regime fell. Al-Zarqawi identified safe houses, stockpiled guns and explosives, and built intelligence networks in Iraq long before the actual invasion by the U.S. and a coalition of allies took place on March 20, 2003.

When Hussein's regime was toppled in May 2003, al-Zarqawi and al Qaeda put their plan into action, launching **insurgent** attacks against the U.S.-led **occupation**. Al-Zarqawi hoped to isolate the Americans by driving all other foreign forces out of Iraq and in this way create a **quagmire** that would lower the morale of the Americans and ultimately force their withdrawal. To do this, al-Zarqawi orchestrated systematic terrorist attacks in Iraq, including the bombing of UN head-quarters in Iraq and the Jordanian embassy in the summer of 2003. Such violence let Americans know that the war would be a bloody one, but U.S. troops struck back with equal ferocity. Al-Zarqawi acknowledged the Americans' tenacity in a 2003 letter to bin Laden and al-Zawahiri, noting, "There is no doubt that Americans' losses are very heavy. But America did not come here only to leave again. There is no doubt that the margin for maneuver has begun to shrink and that the noose around the [insurgents'] throats is growing tighter."

To further destabilize Iraq and create an even more chaotic situation for the coalition—which included combat troops from the U.S., Britain, Australia, and Poland—al-Zarqawi provoked a civil war between Iraq's **Shia** and Sunni Muslims by urging Sunnis to attack the Shia majority. Al-Zarqawi oversaw a series of attacks that included the bombing of Shia shrines, the killing of Shia leaders, and the beheading of hostages. Although al-Zarqawi did achieve his goal of worsening the situation for the U.S.-led coalition in Iraq, by the time al-Zarqawi was killed on June 7, 2006, by an American air strike, the extreme violence that al Qaeda had brought against Shiites and other Iraqi citizens began to turn off many Muslims.

Despite al Qaeda's increasingly unpopular use of violence, the organization still had many followers throughout the Middle East and beyond. In March 2004, bombs exploded on 4 commuter trains in Madrid, Spain, killing 191 and wounding more than 1,800. One year later, in July 2005, four suicide bombers in London, England, blew themselves up—3 on the city's underground trains and 1 on a city bus—killing 56 people and wounding 700. Although no connection was proven between the perpetrators of either attack and al Qaeda, the attacks' similarity to those orchestrated by al Qaeda suggested that al Qaeda was spreading its jihadist ideology across the globe and had a major influence

The 2004 Madrid train bombings occurred during the morning rush hour, when the terrorists knew the death toll was likely to be highest.

On July 6, 2005, Britons celebrated London's selection as host of the 2012 Olympics; the next day, they mourned the bombing attacks in the city.

on new terrorist cells. The number of known al Qaeda-affiliated terrorist cells worldwide would reach 40 by 2010.

In Afghanistan, meanwhile, the Taliban continued to grow stronger. The group, operating increasingly from Pakistan, became more violent, using guerrilla tactics, suicide bombings, and bombs planted along roadways to try to create chaos in Afghanistan and Pakistan and drive out coalition forces. The newly democratic and U.S.-supported Afghan government, led by president Hamid Karzai, did not have adequate security forces to allow effective self-governance and faced charges of corruption (including that government officials and police officers accepted bribes from drug lords). The Taliban took full advantage of these problems by offering high wages to any young Muslim willing to join its ranks. Poor and mistrustful of their new government, some Afghanis chose to accept the Taliban's offers, even if they did not agree with Taliban policies.

ROOT OF WAR

In a November 2009 report released by the charity Oxfam America, 70 percent of Afghans said that poverty, not the Taliban or corruption within the national government, was the main cause of war in their country. The report, based on a survey of more than 700 people, suggested that poor living conditions and unemployment had a bigger role than politics in destabilizing the country. Nearly 50 percent cited the corruption and the ineffectiveness of their newly created, democratic government as the main reasons for continued fighting, and 36 percent said the Taliban was to blame.

CHAPTER FOUR

A DIFFICULT WAR

With the initial success of Operation Enduring Freedom in the fall of 2001, the U.S. and its allies seemed on track to achieving their goal of defeating al Qaeda and the Taliban. And with the unexpected support from Pakistan, the U.S. was beginning to realize its goal of getting other nations, such as Libya, to end state sponsorship of terrorism. The U.S. received support from many Western nations, especially Britain, and even won sympathy from citizens of some Middle Eastern nations, including many young people in Iran who were tired of the repressed society under the mullahs (teachers of Islamic law) that had existed since the Iranian Revolution of 1979. But when the coalition had the Taliban and key al Qaeda leaders seemingly trapped in the mountains along the Pakistan-Afghanistan border in 2002, the U.S. diverted its attention to Iraq.

Ever since the end of the Persian Gulf War in 1991, when Saddam Hussein was forced to leave Kuwait but allowed to remain president of Iraq, Western nations, especially the U.S., had been wary of his unpredictable behavior. After his defeat in 1991, the UN—in order to limit his ability to threaten other nations—passed resolutions forcing him to destroy all WMD and all missiles that had a range of more than 93 miles (150 km). When Hussein repeatedly

Iranian president Mahmoud Ahmadinejad insisted he was against building nuclear weapons, stating that it was "illegal and against our religion."

AXIS OF EVIL

During the lead-up to America's 2003 invasion of Iraq, U.S. president George W. Bush, in his January 2002 State of the Union address, described Iraq, Iran, and North Korea as an "axis of evil." He said that the governments of these countries supported terrorism and might one day sell WMD—including nuclear bombs—to terrorists, making the three nations a danger to the world. In 2009, Iranian president Mahmoud Ahmadinejad admitted that Iran was stockpiling uranium (which can be used in building nuclear weapons) but asserted that it was only for the production of energy.

George W. Bush and Tony Blair were
closely allied, continuing the historical
"Special Relationship" that has existed
between the U.S. and Britain.

refused to allow UN weapons inspectors into Iraq to see if he had complied with the order, the UN placed sanctions on Iraq, which restricted Iraq's ability to trade with other nations and caused shortages of food and medical care for the Iraqi people.

After the 9/11 attacks, President Bush and his administration decided that Hussein's noncompliance could no longer be tolerated—that, after bin Laden, Hussein represented the biggest threat to global peace and freedom. In February 2003, U.S. secretary of state Colin Powell presented evidence to the UN Security Council suggesting that al-Zarqawi and the rest of al Qaeda were allies and partners of Hussein's. The Bush administration was also convinced that Hussein still possessed WMD, which he could use at any moment against his Middle Eastern neighbors or Western nations. "No nation can possibly claim that Iraq has disarmed," Bush said in a March 2003 address. "And it will not disarm so long as Saddam Hussein holds power. The security of the world requires disarming Saddam Hussein now." British prime minister Tony Blair shared those same fears. Despite not receiving UN approval, and against the advice of the governments of many countries, the U.S.—supported by troops from Britain, Australia, Denmark, Spain, and Poland—invaded Iraq in March 2003.

However, when American troops captured the capital city of Baghdad in May, the U.S. found no hard evidence linking Hussein's regime to al Qaeda. In addition,

WMD—on which much of the invasion's justification was based—
were never found, despite a thorough, year-long search of Iraqi
military compounds. Complicating the conflict further, what little
international support the U.S. and its allies had for the war in Iraq
waned as Iraqi insurgents stepped up their deadly attacks throughout
the next few years, keeping much of the country in a state of chaos.
Coalition troops launched counterattacks in an attempt to restore
order, and thousands of civilians died amid the violence.

As battles raged in Iraq, Afghanistan proved to be just as problem-
atic. In 2007, six years after the U.S. sent al Qaeda and Taliban leaders into hiding, a total of 140 suicide bombing operations occurred
in Afghanistan, and more Americans died from enemy attacks that
year than in any previous year. The key for future U.S. strategy in the
War on Terror, said counterterrorism specialist Marc Sageman, was to
base the war on ideas rather than on solely military operations. "The
difficult task," Sageman noted, "is preventing a future generation
from joining this violent terrorist movement and doing more dam-
age." Despite increased Pakistani security, the Taliban grew more

Iraqi citizens look on as U.S. soldiers move through Baghdad in 2003 in a search for weapons or bomb-making materials.

IRAQ'S INDEPENDENCE

In August 2009, insurgents took advantage of the U.S. troop withdrawal from Iraqi cities by increasing their attacks, killing 456 people (the highest 1-month death toll in 13 months). Nevertheless, in the summer of 2010, U.S. president Barack Obama oversaw a scheduled reduction of American troops in Iraq, from 77,500 in July to 50,000 by September, with plans to remove the last remaining troops by December 2011. While many Americans applauded the pullout, some U.S. officials remained concerned that the loss of troops could destabilize Iraq.

UNITED NATIONS

Since its founding in 1945, the United Nations (a term first used by U.S. president Franklin D. Roosevelt to describe the Allied nations during World War II) has promoted peace among the various countries of the world. The UN works to facilitate cooperation in international law, security, economic development, social progress, human rights, and the achievement of world peace. As of 2011, the UN included 192 member states.

U.S. president Barack Obama, who pledged to set a new course for the war, visited U.S. troops in Iraq shortly after taking office in 2009.

powerful in Pakistan as well and was responsible for nearly 60 suicide operations within that country in 2007. U.S. officials believed the al Qaeda-Taliban connection was responsible for the murder of former Pakistani prime minister Benazir Bhutto in December 2007. A lack of coordination between U.S. forces and troops from the **North Atlantic Treaty Organization's (NATO)** International Security Assistance Forces (ISAF) also gave Taliban militants more breathing room.

Benazir Bhutto

In hindsight, it seemed that the U.S. had traded the possibility of a quick and thorough victory in Afghanistan in 2002 for its parallel invasion of Iraq in 2003, which loosened the noose around al Qaeda and the Taliban. When newly elected U.S. president Barack Obama was sworn into office in January 2009, he faced a worsening situation in Afghanistan, the loss of British support in Iraq (after Blair's replacement as prime minister by Gordon Brown in June 2007), and increasing calls from the American people and many members of Congress for

HUNGER STRIKES

In 2004, reports of alleged prisoner abuse at the hands of U.S. military personnel emerged from America's Guantánamo Bay detention camp (where many terror suspects and other captured war combatants were held). Detainees claimed to have been beaten, exposed to extreme temperatures, and deprived of medical treatment. In protest of these alleged abuses, some detainees went on hunger strikes. One of the biggest strikes took place from June through July 2005, when nearly 200 detainees fasted. The strike ended after some prison reforms were made and after guards force-fed many detainees to bring them back to health.

American combat troops left Iraq in the summer of 2010, leaving the rebuilding nation primarily in the hands of the new Iraqi government and military.

a U.S. troop withdrawal from both countries. In keeping with a campaign promise, Obama began large-scale withdrawals from Iraq in the summer of 2010, vowing to remove the last of the U.S. troops by December 2011. He also promised to begin to withdraw troops from Afghanistan by July 2011. U.S. officials hoped that the death of bin Laden—who was found and killed by U.S. Navy SEALs in May 2011 in a raid that made global headlines—would reduce the influence of al Qaeda and the Taliban in Afghanistan.

Although, to many Americans, the 9/11 attacks seemed to come out of nowhere, the seeds of the conflict that ultimately turned into the War on Terror were planted long before 2001. The downfall of the Ottoman Empire, the creation of Israel, fundamental religious differences, the increasing global influence of affluent Western nations—all of these factors and more created a gulf between the nations of the West and fundamentalist segments of the Islamic world. Al Qaeda was born, Westerners learned the word "jihad," and terrorists struck at the heart of America. The causes of the war have become clear, but as the conflict enters a new decade, its resolution remains a challenge.

caliphate — an Islamic form of government led by a head of state called a caliph; a goal of many Islamic extremists is to establish a caliphate throughout the world's Islamic-majority countries

cleric — a religious leader or priest; in the context of the War on Terror, the term usually refers to an Islamic cleric

coalition — an alliance of individuals or groups who join together for a common cause

diplomats — people who participate in non-hostile negotiations or interactions carried out between countries working toward alliances, treaties, or agreements

extremists — people who hold views that are radical or far from the traditional or common view

fatwa — a binding edict, or order, given by an Islamic religious leader; Osama bin Laden's 1998 fatwa against the West was not a fatwa in the truest sense, as he did not meet the qualifications for a religious leader

genocide — the deliberate extermination or destruction of a group of people based on their ethnicity, culture, or political beliefs

infidels — people who do not accept a particular religious faith; it is a term especially used by Muslims as a reference to people who do not believe in Islam

insurgent — describing fighters who partake in a revolt or uprising against a government or ruling force

intelligence — information concerning political or military matters, including potential acts by an enemy or possible enemy

jihad — a holy war waged by Muslims as a religious duty against people who do not believe in Islam

Kurdish — describing people who inhabit parts of Syria, Iran, Iraq, Turkey, and the former Soviet Union; Kurds have different cultural customs and speak a different language from other Muslims, and they have fought for many years to have an independent nation

militants — people who use aggression or combat in support of a cause

North Atlantic Treaty Organization (NATO) — an alliance of 28 countries in North America and Europe that provides political or military support to protect its member countries

nuclear — pertaining to or involving atomic weapons, bombs or missiles with enormous destructive power derived from the uncontrolled splitting or combining of atoms

occupation — the holding and control of an area by a foreign military or force

Pentagon — a huge, five-sided building near Washington, D.C., that is the headquarters of the U.S. Department of Defense

quagmire — a difficult or precarious situation that is very difficult to resolve or escape

secular — being void of religious ties or affiliations

Shia — a sect, or group, of Muslims who believe the prophet Muhammad designated his son-in-law, Ali ibn Abi Talib, as his successor; Shiites make up about 20 percent of Muslims worldwide

Sunni — a sect, or group, of Muslims who proclaimed Abu Bakr, a prominent disciple of the prophet Muhammad, as Muhammad's successor; Sunnis make up about 80 percent of Muslims worldwide

UN Security Council — a body of the UN composed of representatives from 15 countries; the Security Council can pass resolutions that authorize war or impose economic penalties upon countries

weapons of mass destruction (WMD) — weapons such as nuclear bombs and chemicals or gases that are capable of killing large numbers of people or destroying huge areas

ENDNOTES

Cole, David. *Justice at War: The Men and Ideas That Shaped America's War on Terror*. New York: New York Review Books, 2008.

Habeck, Mary. *Knowing the Enemy: Jihadist Ideology and the War on Terror*. New Haven, Conn.: Yale University Press, 2006.

Hiro, Dilip. *War without End: The Rise of Islamist Terrorism and Global Response*. New York: Routledge, 2002.

Khosrokhavar, Farhad. *Inside Jihadism: Understanding Jihadi Movements Worldwide*. Boulder, Colo.: Paradigm Publishers, 2009.

SELECTED BIBLIOGRAPHY

National Commission on Terrorist Attacks Upon the United States. *The 9/11 Commission Report: Final Report of the National Commission on Terrorist Attacks upon the United States*. New York: W. W. Norton, 2004.

Rashid, Ahmed. *Descent into Chaos: The U.S. and the Disaster in Pakistan, Afghanistan, and Central Asia*. New York: Penguin, 2008.

Riedel, Bruce. *The Search for al Qaeda: Its Leadership, Ideology, and Future*. Washington, D.C.: Brookings Institution Press, 2008.

Russell, Malcolm B. *The Middle East and South Asia*. 42nd ed. Harpers Ferry, W. Va.: Stryker-Post Publications, 2008.

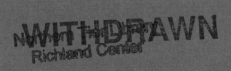